Colorful Sight LLC

This Book Belongs To:

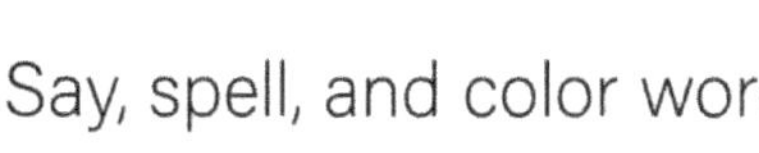

Say, spell, and color word.

Circle the correct spelling in the box.

the eth hte
het the het
eht teh
the teh the

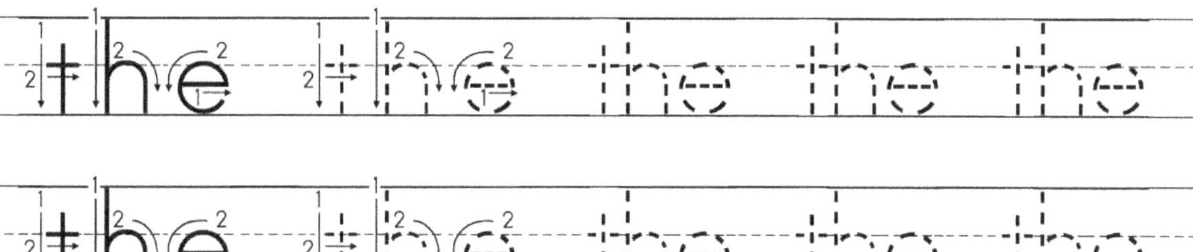

Fill in the blank with the sight word.

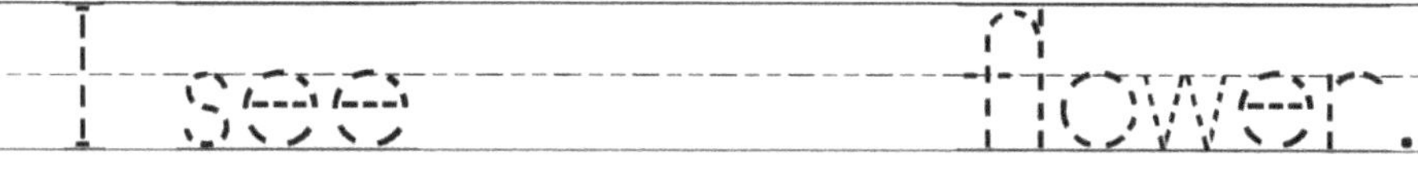

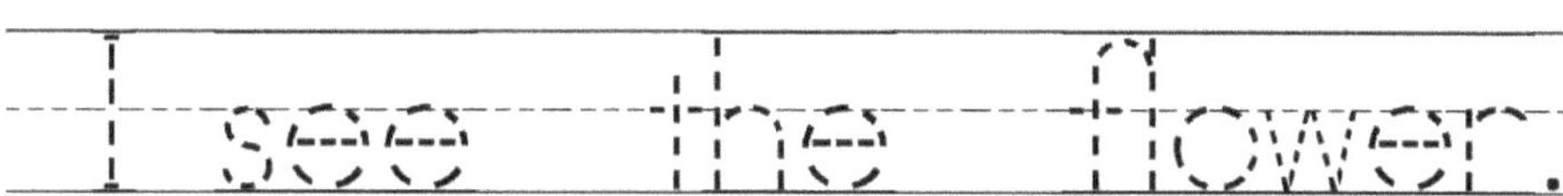

Fill in each box to make the sight word.

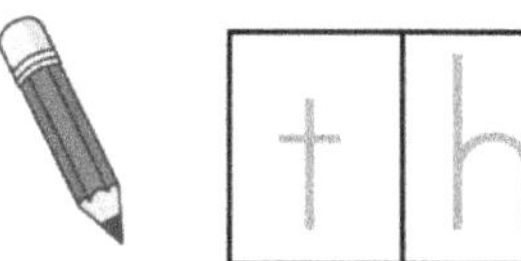

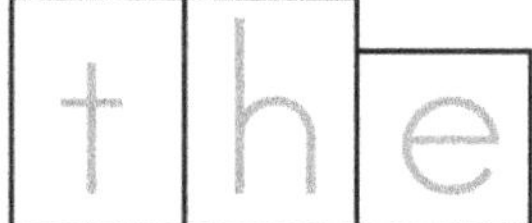

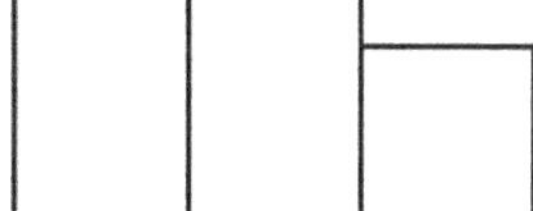

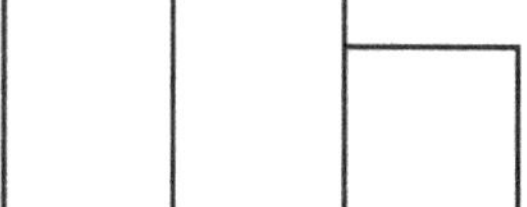

she

Say, spell, and color word.

Circle the correct spelling in the box.

she ehs hes
hes she
she seh she
ehs she seh

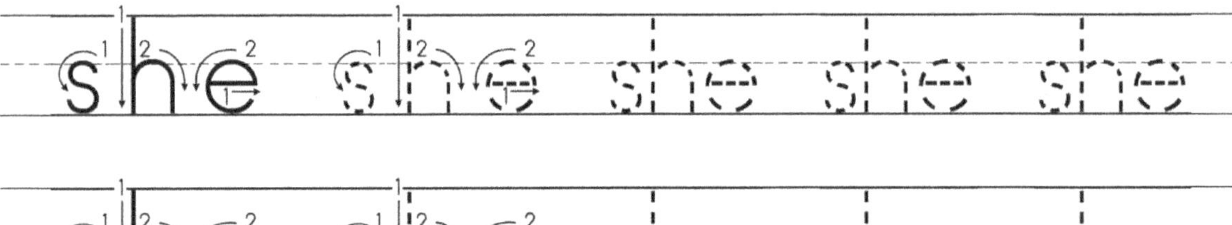

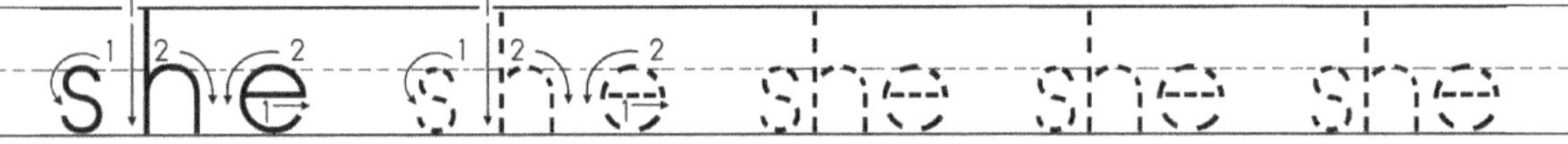

Fill in the blank with the sight word.

_______ likes unicorns.

She likes unicorns.

Fill in each box to make the sight word.

 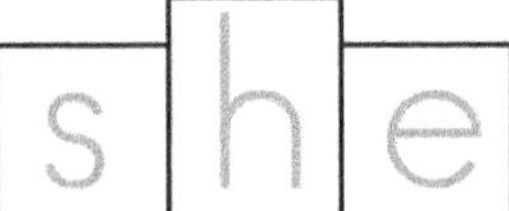

s h e

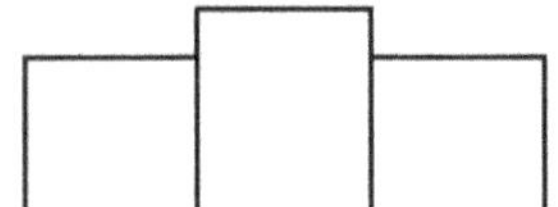

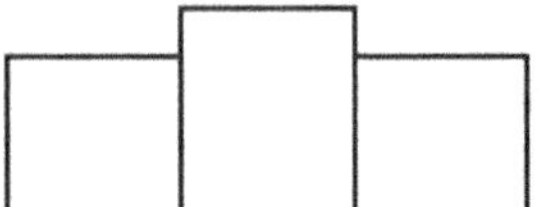

get

 Say, spell, and color word.

Circle the correct spelling in the box.

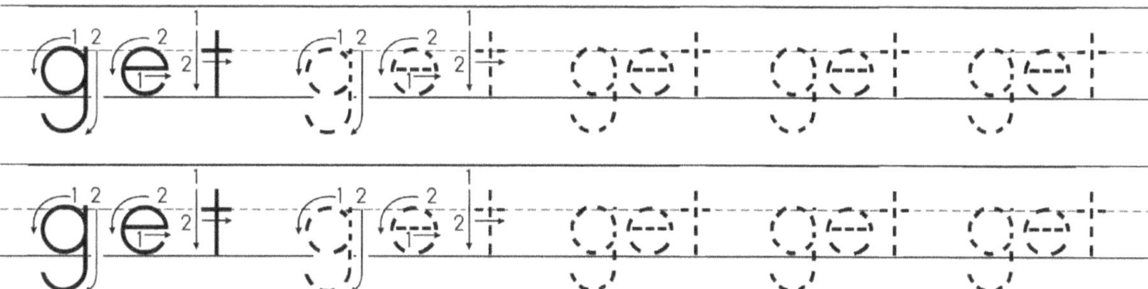

 Fill in the blank with the sight word.

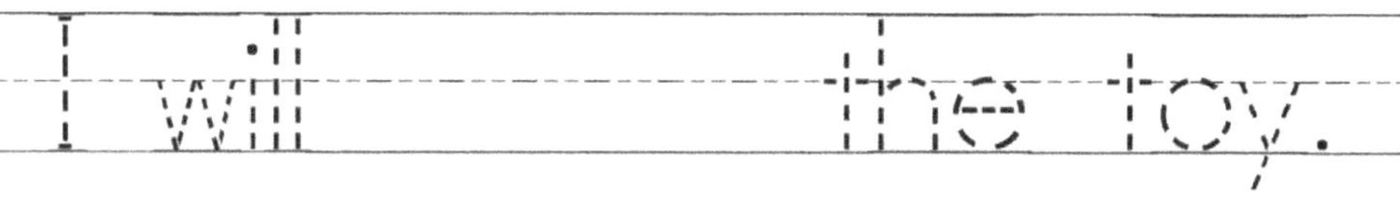

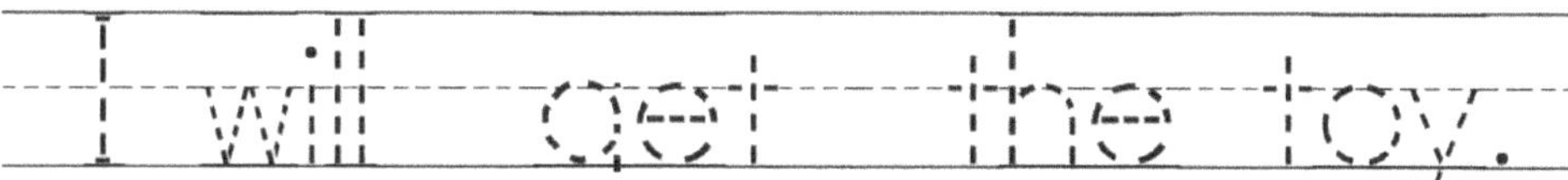

Fill in each box to make the sight word.

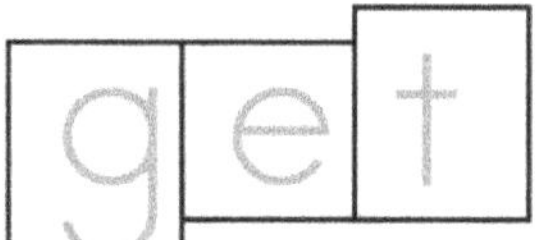 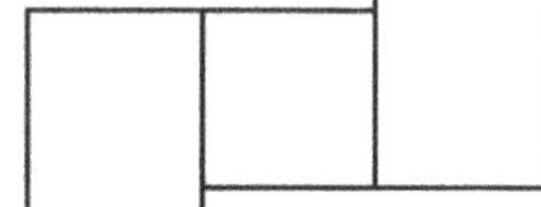 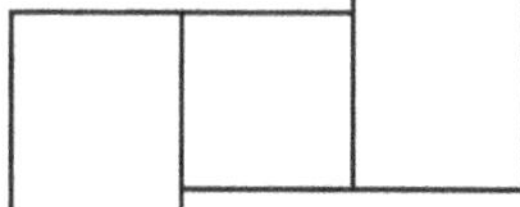

and

Say, spell, and color word.

Circle the correct spelling in the box.

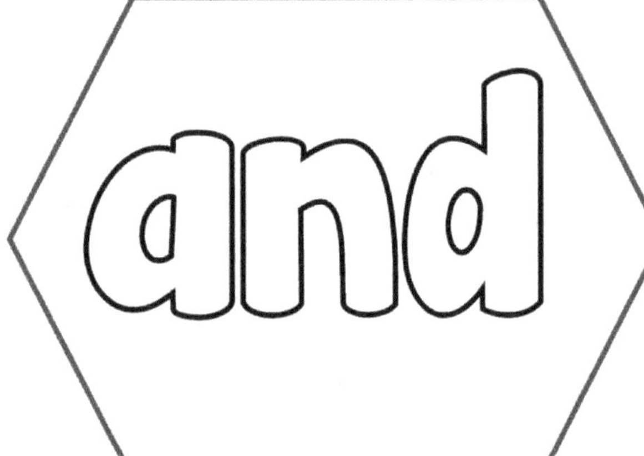

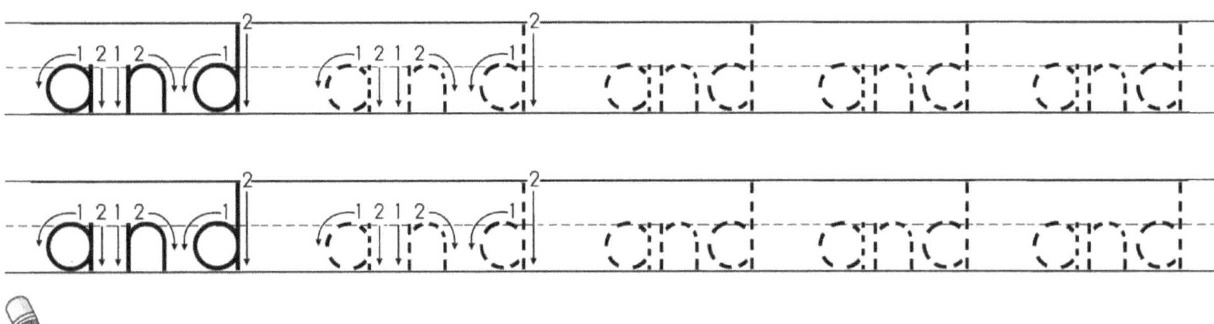

Fill in the blank with the sight word.

I eat cookies __________ chips.

I eat cookies and chips.

Fill in each box to make the sight word.

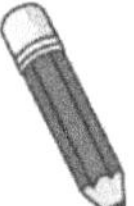
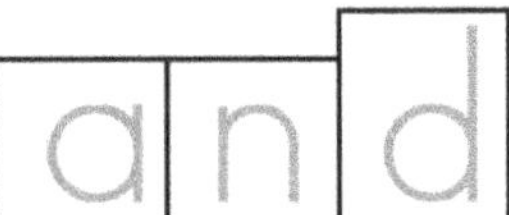

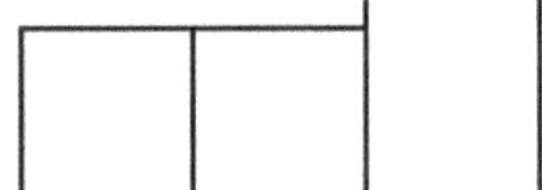
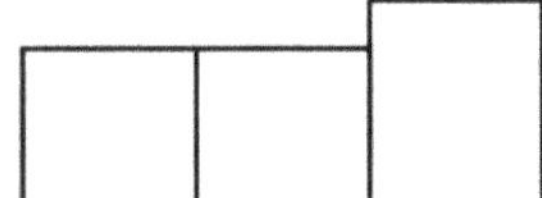

Say, spell, and color word.

Circle the correct spelling in the box.

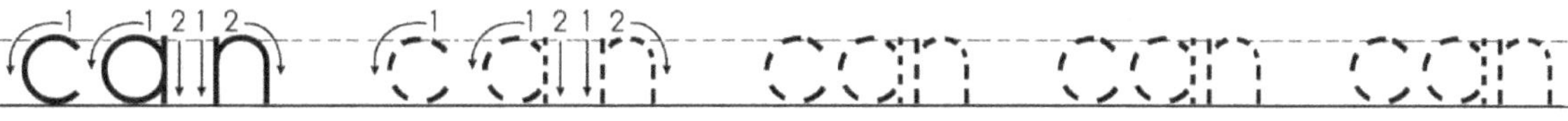

can can can can can

can can can can can

Fill in the blank with the sight word.

I __________ climb a tree.

I can climb a tree.

Fill in each box to make the sight word.

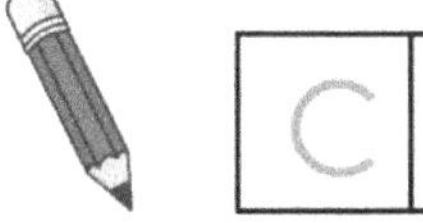   

Say, spell, and color word.

Circle the correct spelling in the box.

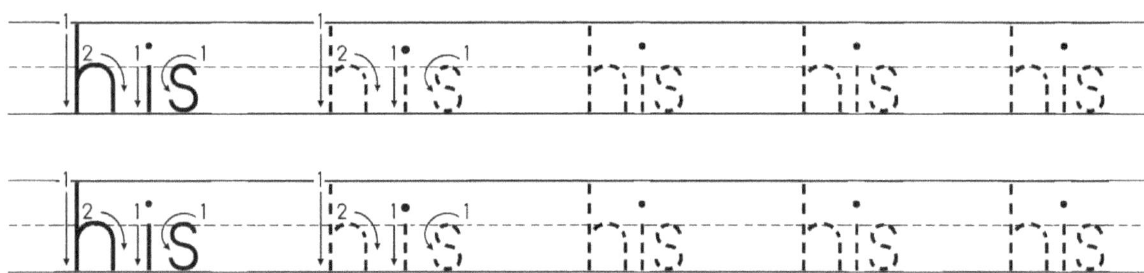

his   his   his   his   his

his   his   his   his   his

Fill in the blank with the sight word.

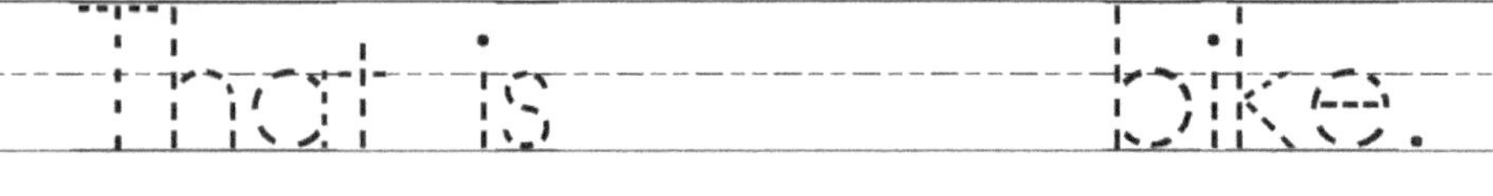

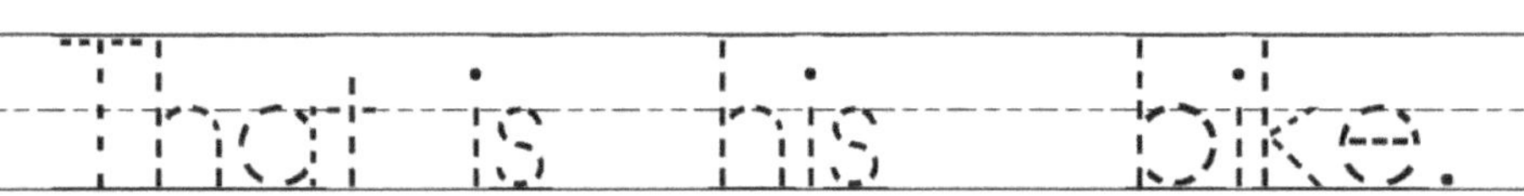

Fill in each box to make the sight word.

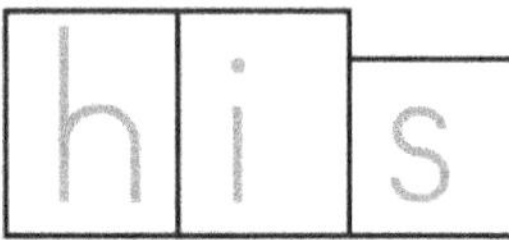

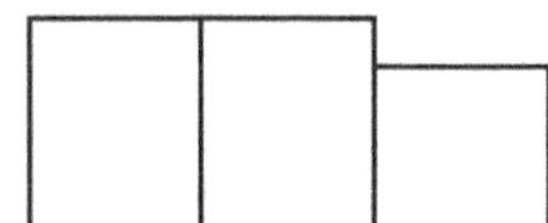
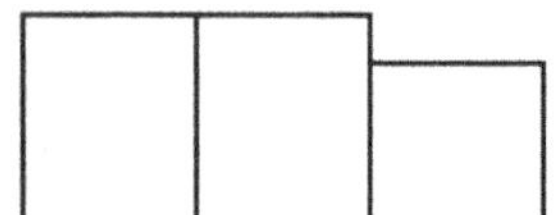

for

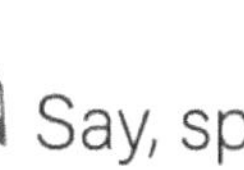

Say, spell, and color word.

Circle the correct spelling in the box.

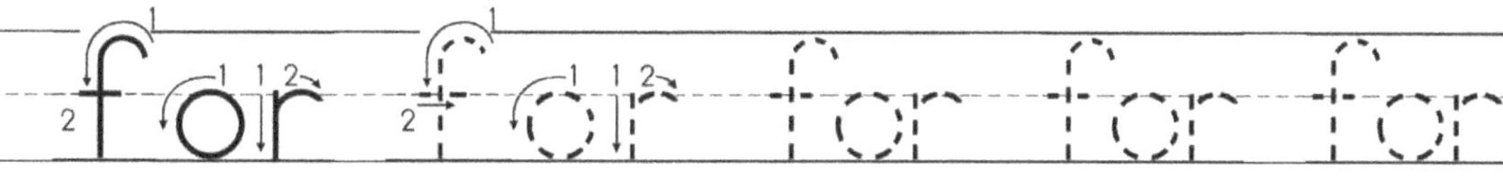

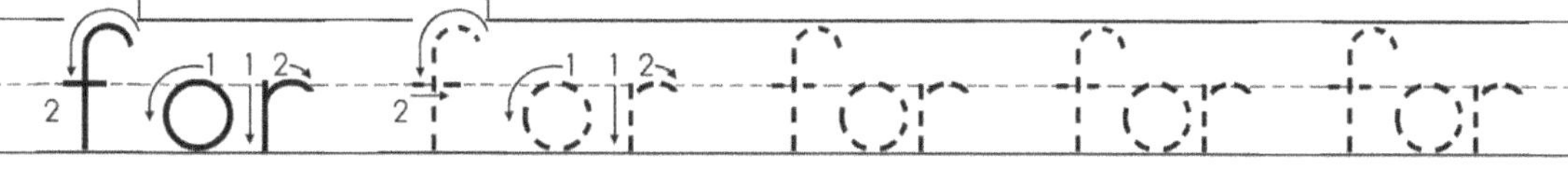

Fill in the blank with the sight word.

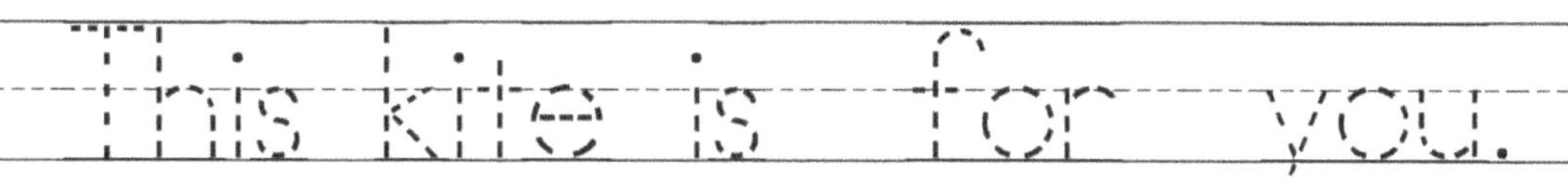

Fill in each box to make the sight word.

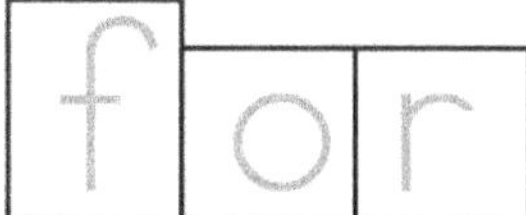
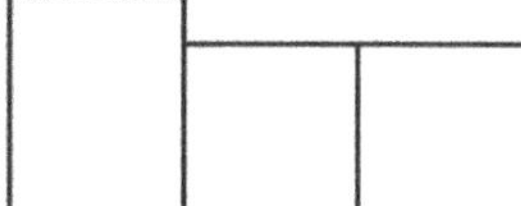
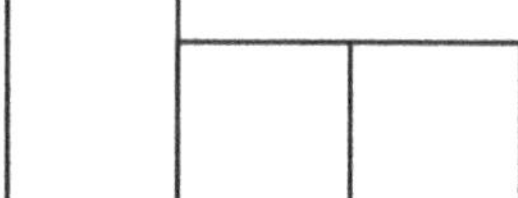

Say, spell, and color word.　　　　Circle the correct spelling in the box.

all　　ala　　all
lla　　all　　aal　　ala
lal
all　　aal　　all　　lal

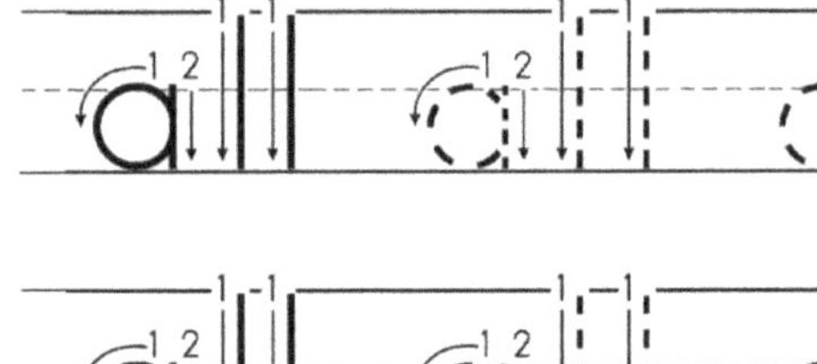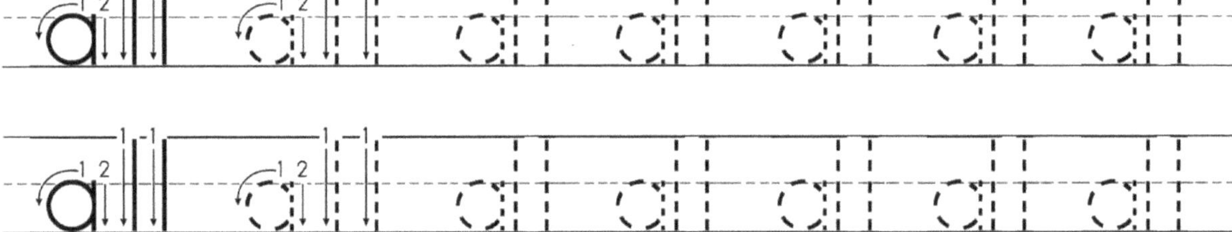

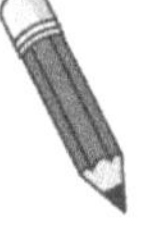

Fill in the blank with the sight word.

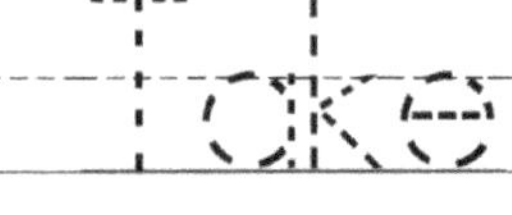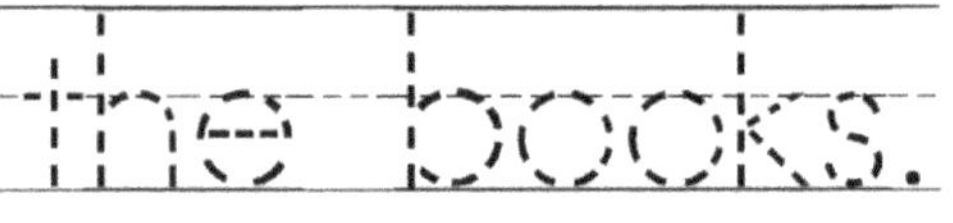

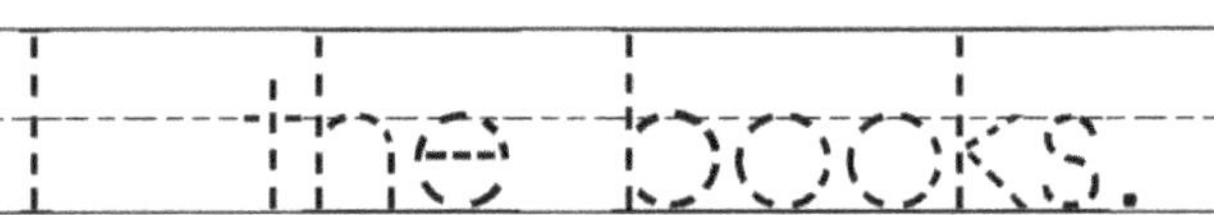

Fill in each box to make the sight word.

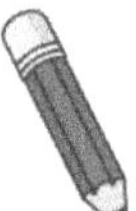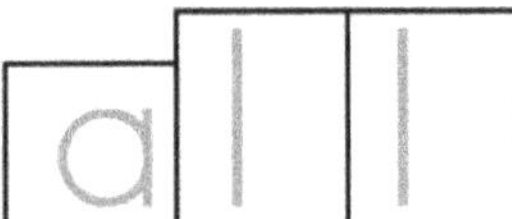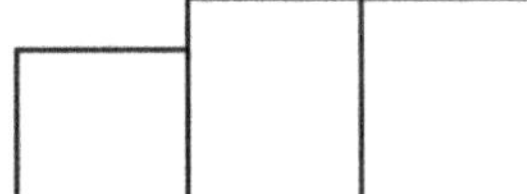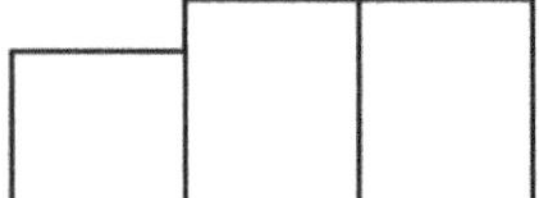

are

Say, spell, and color word.

Circle the correct spelling in the box.

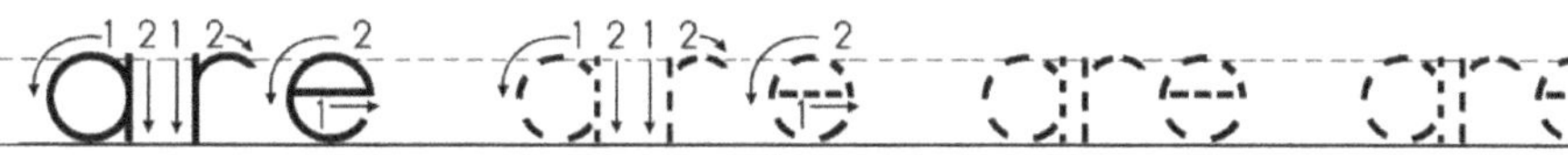

Fill in the blank with the sight word.

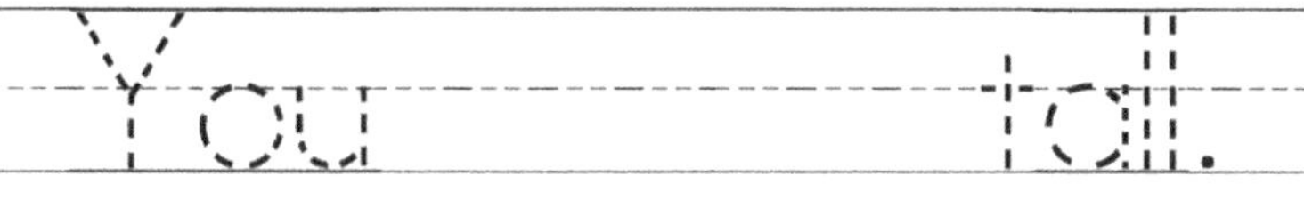

Fill in each box to make the sight word.

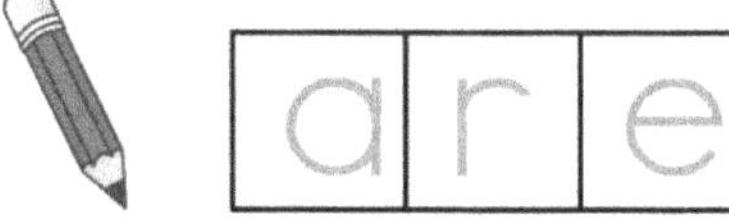

did

Say, spell, and color word.

Circle the correct spelling in the box.

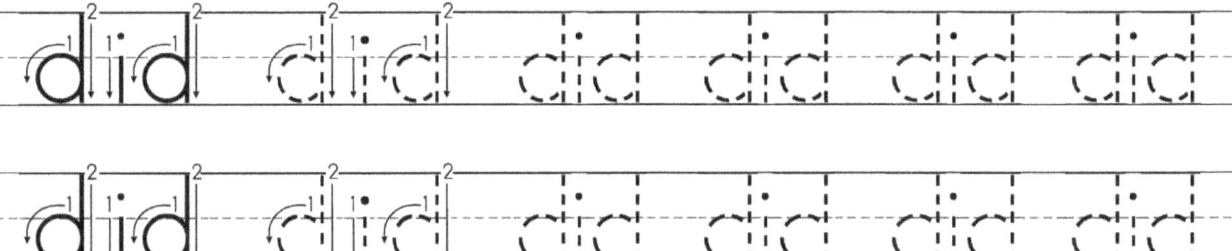

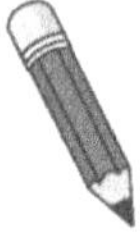

Fill in the blank with the sight word.

We _______ our homework.

We did our homework.

Fill in each box to make the sight word.

 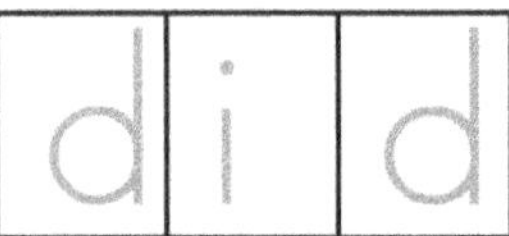 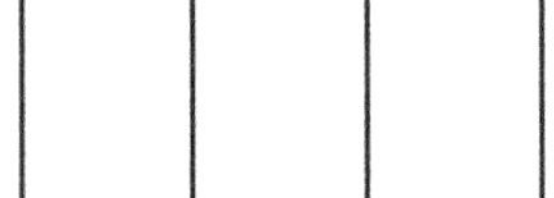 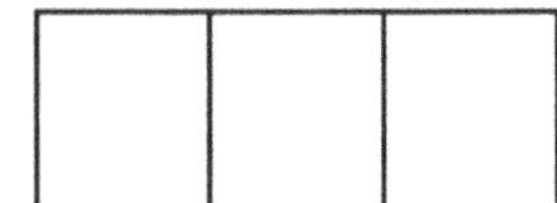

saw

 Say, spell, and color word.

Circle the correct spelling in the box.

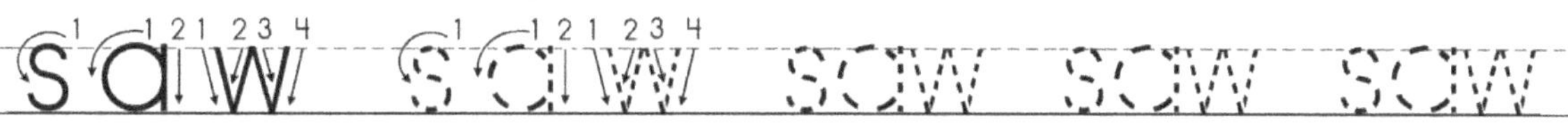

 Fill in the blank with the sight word.

My mom _______ a star.

My mom saw a star.

Fill in each box to make the sight word.

s	a	w

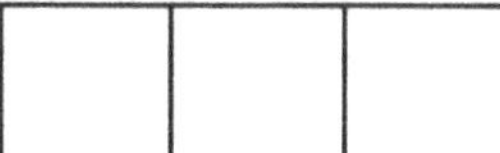

Say, spell, and color word.

Circle the correct spelling in the box.

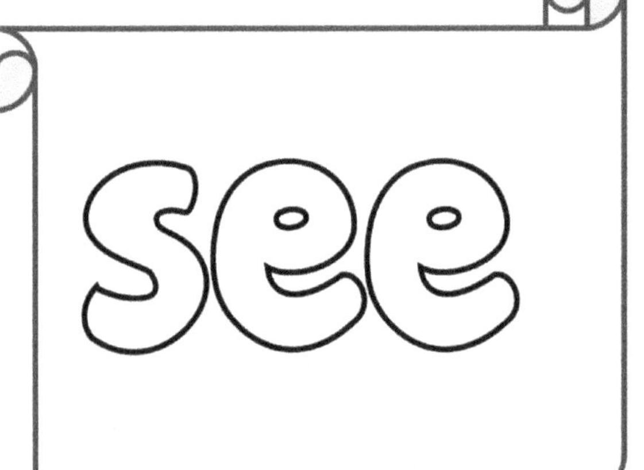

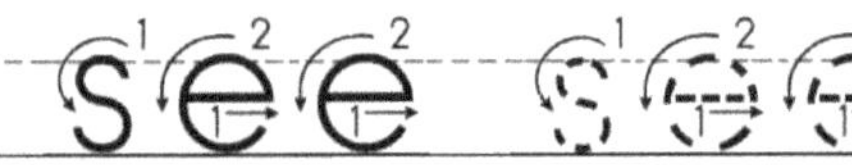

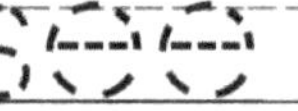

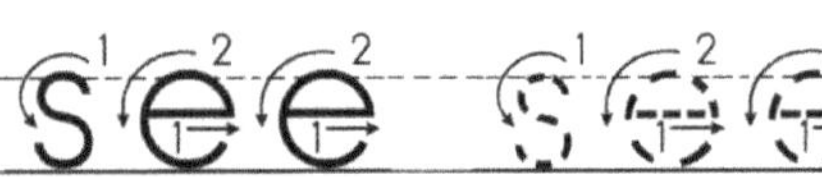
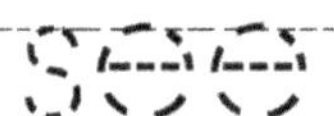

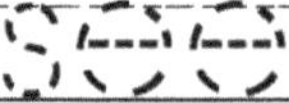

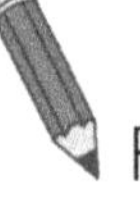

Fill in the blank with the sight word.

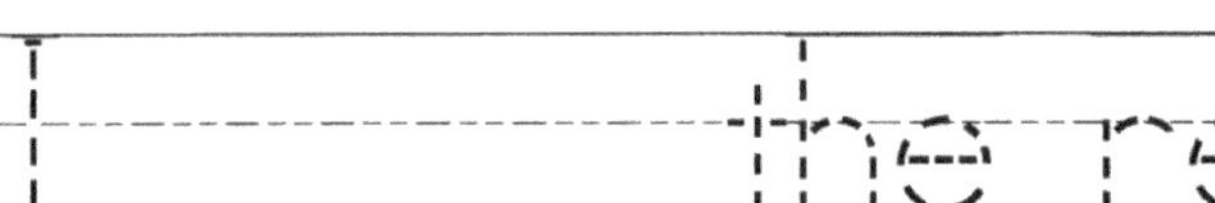

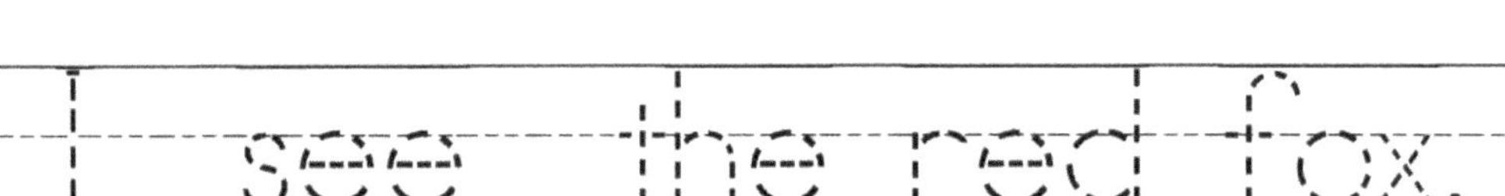

Fill in each box to make the sight word.

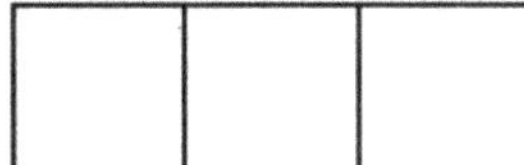
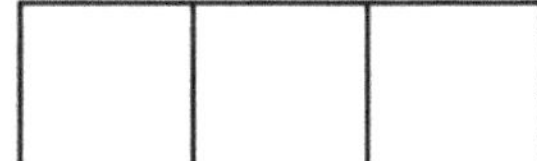

eat

Say, spell, and color word.

Circle the correct spelling in the box.

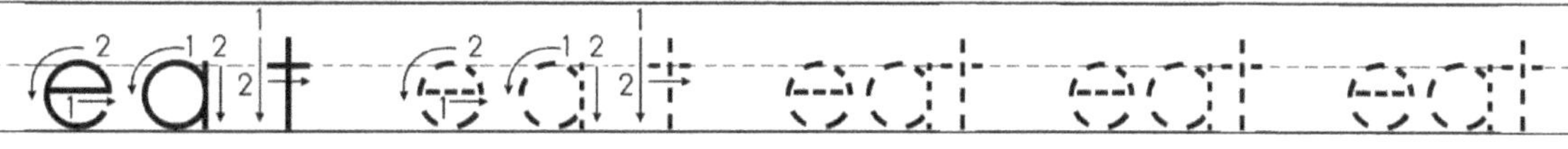

Fill in the blank with the sight word.

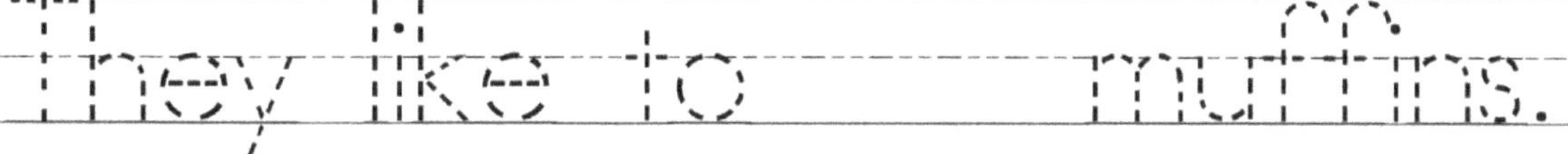

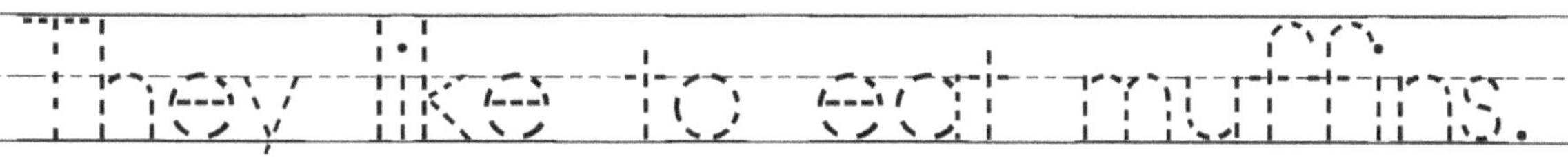

Fill in each box to make the sight word.

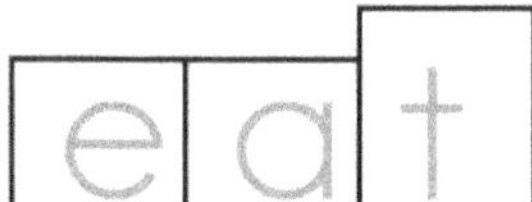

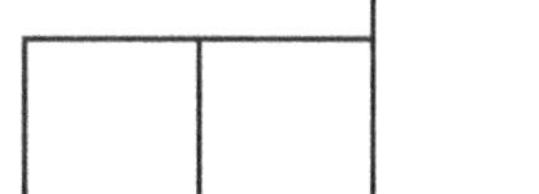
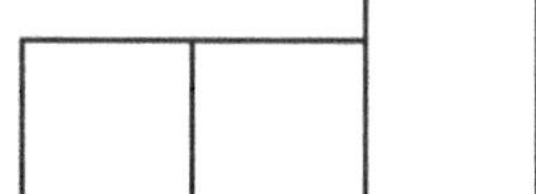

will

Say, spell, and color word.

Circle the correct spelling in the box.

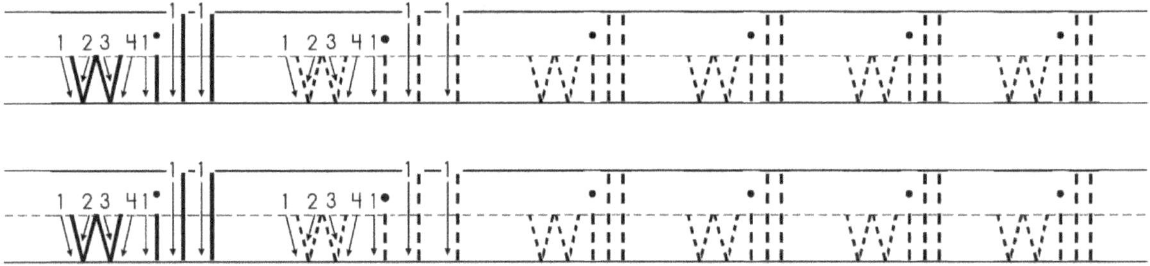

Fill in the blank with the sight word.

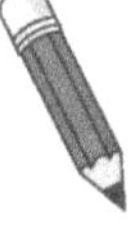

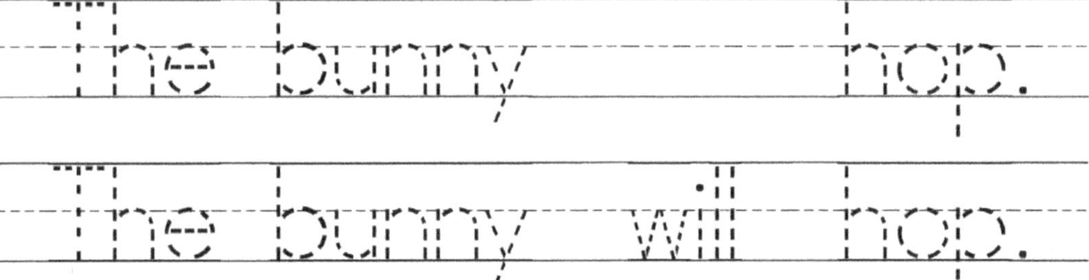

Fill in each box to make the sight word.

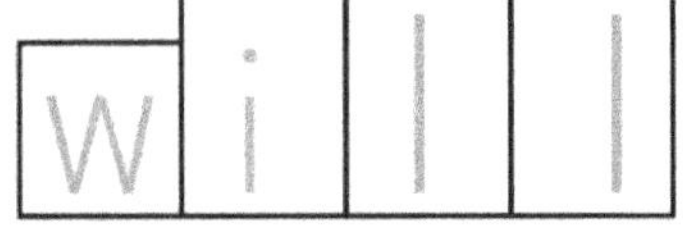

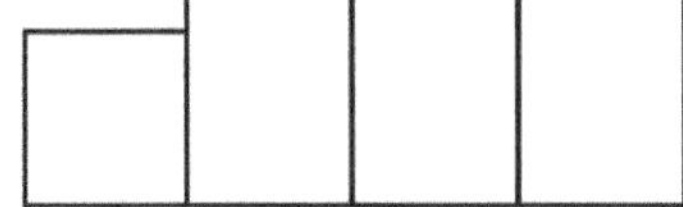
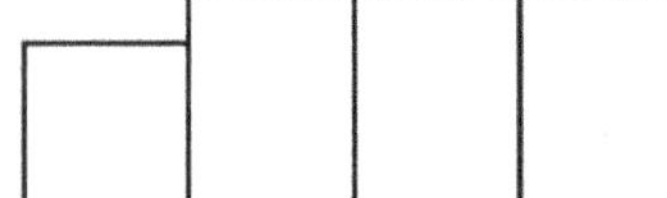

was

Say, spell, and color word.

Circle the correct spelling in the box.

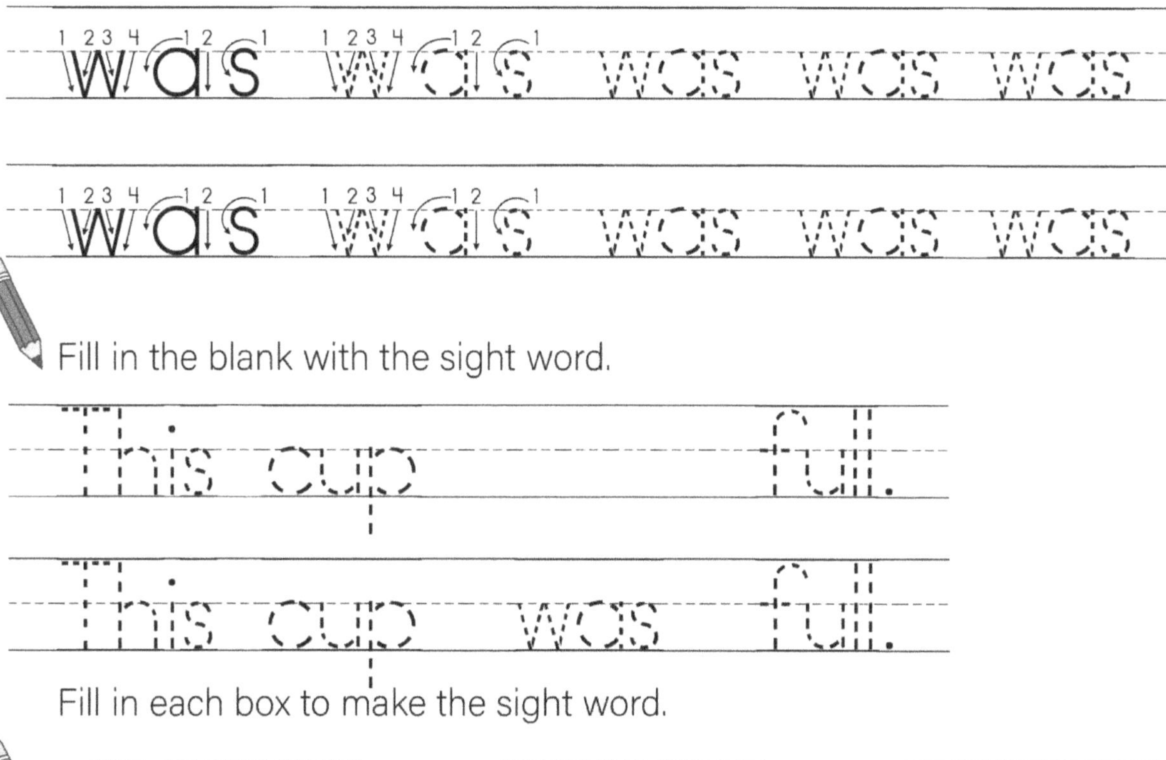

was was was was was

was was was was was

Fill in the blank with the sight word.

This cup _____ full.

This cup was full.

Fill in each box to make the sight word.

w a s

you

Circle the correct spelling in the box.

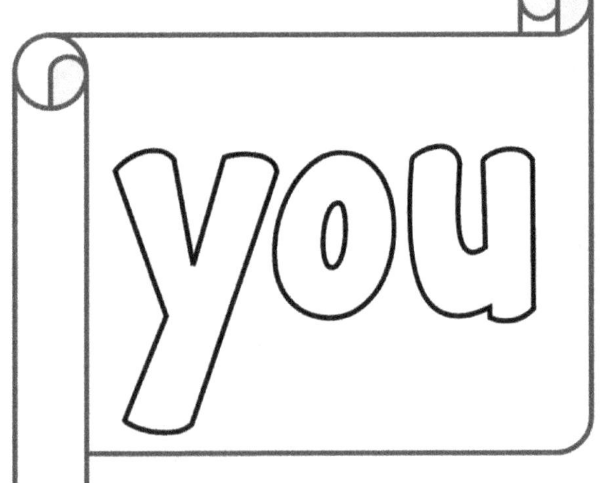

you you you you you

you you you you you

Fill in the blank with the sight word.

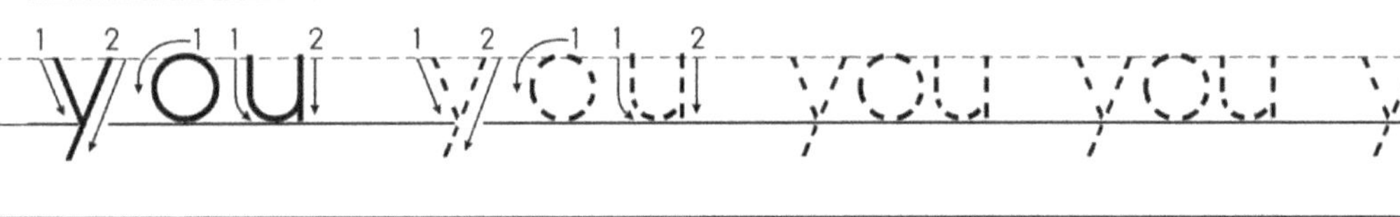

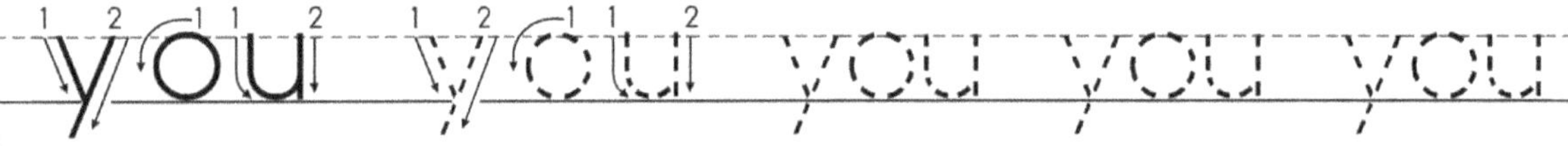

Fill in each box to make the sight word.

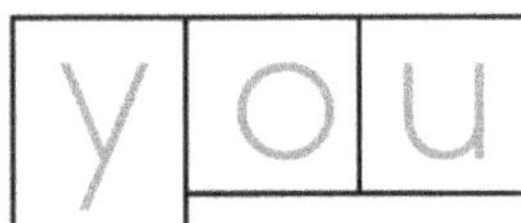

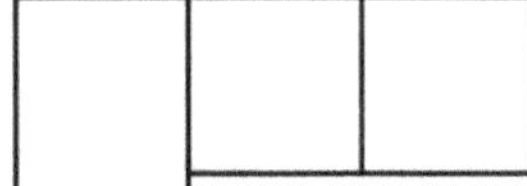

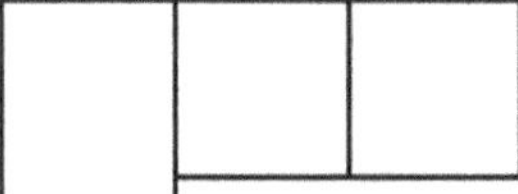

too

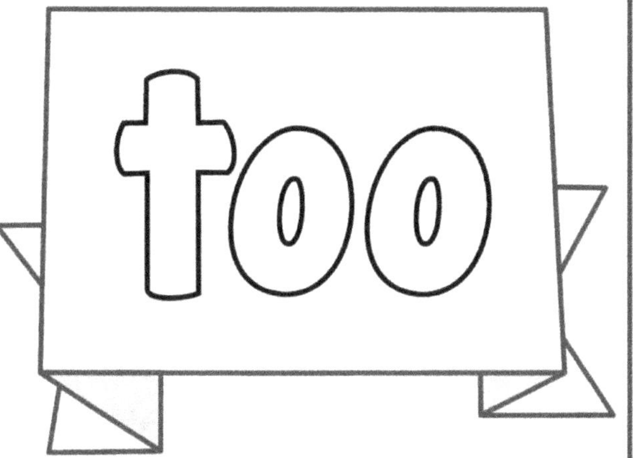

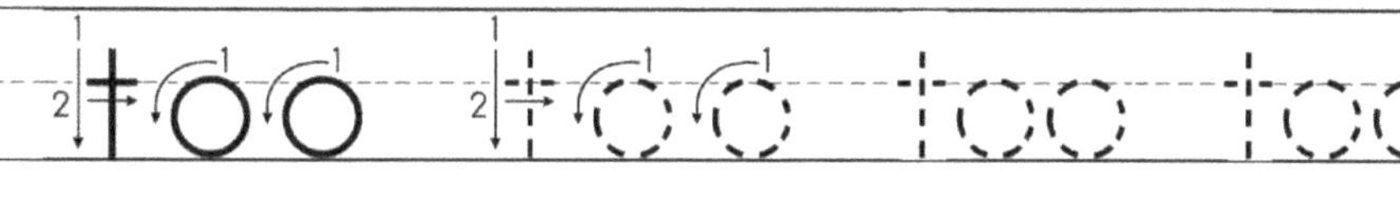

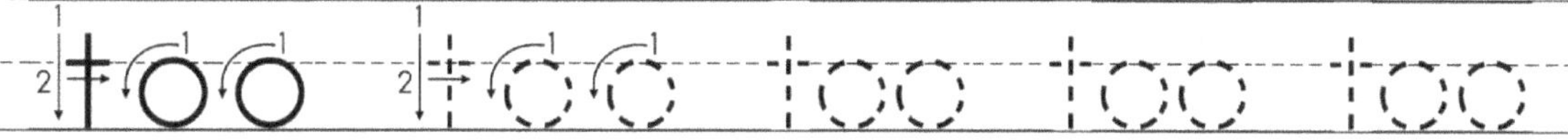

Fill in the blank with the sight word.

She can jump ___________ .

She can jump too.

Fill in each box to make the sight word.

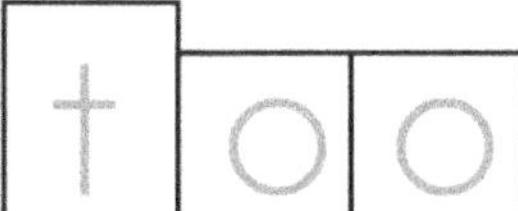
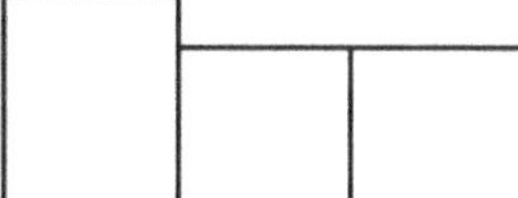
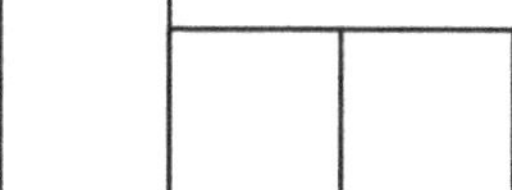

now

Say, spell, and color word.

Circle the correct spelling in the box.

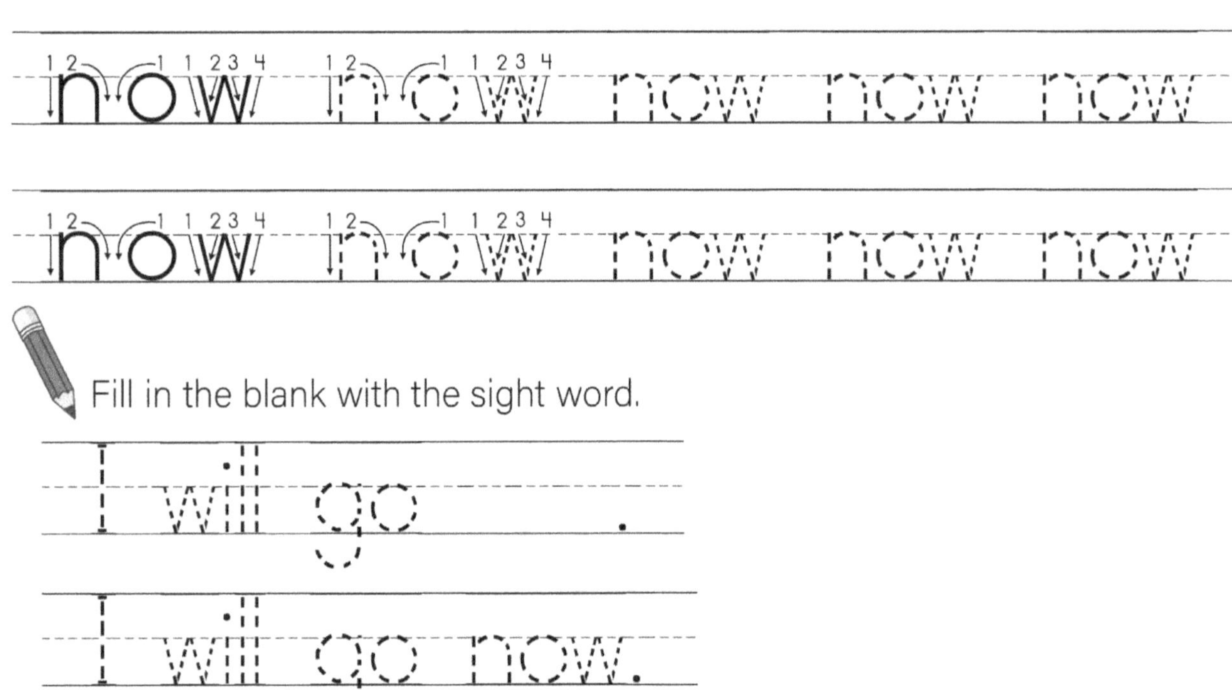

now now now now now

now now now now now

Fill in the blank with the sight word.

I will go ____ .

I will go now.

Fill in each box to make the sight word.

n o w

who

Say, spell, and color word.

Circle the correct spelling in the box.

woh   who   owh
who   woh   ohw
how   who
woh   ohw   who

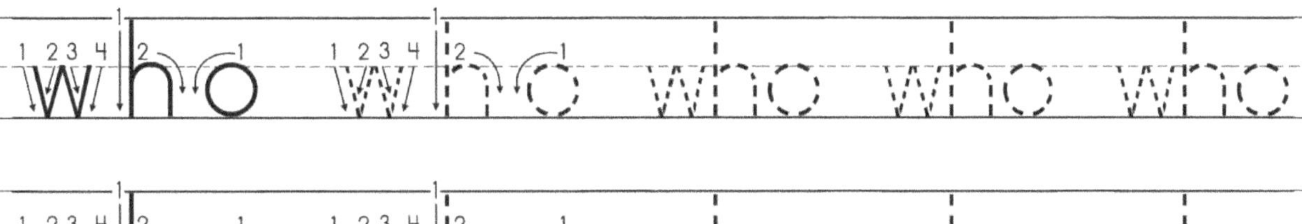

1 2 3 4 who 1 2 3 4 who who who who

1 2 3 4 who 1 2 3 4 who who who who

Fill in the blank with the sight word.

_______ wants ice cream?

Who wants ice cream?

Fill in each box to make the sight word.

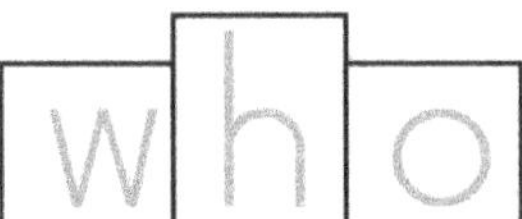

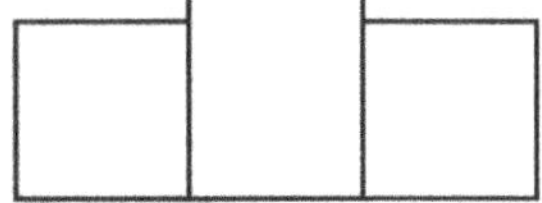
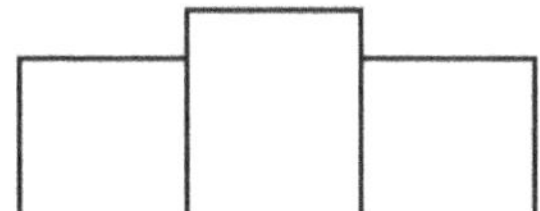

our

Say, spell, and color word.

Circle the correct spelling in the box.

ruo   oru   our
our   uro   ruo
uor   uro   our
our   rou   oru

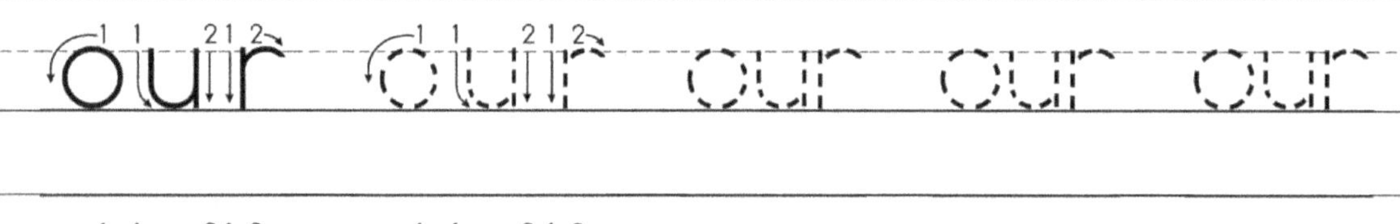

Fill in the blank with the sight word.

This is _____ seat.

This is our seat.

Fill in each box to make the sight word.

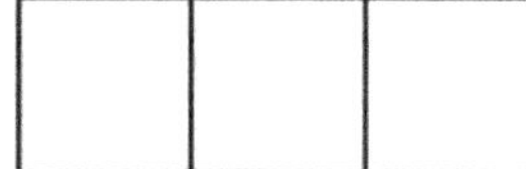

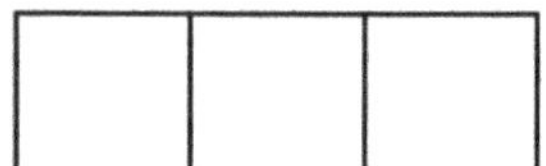

not

Say, spell, and color word.

Circle the correct spelling in the box.

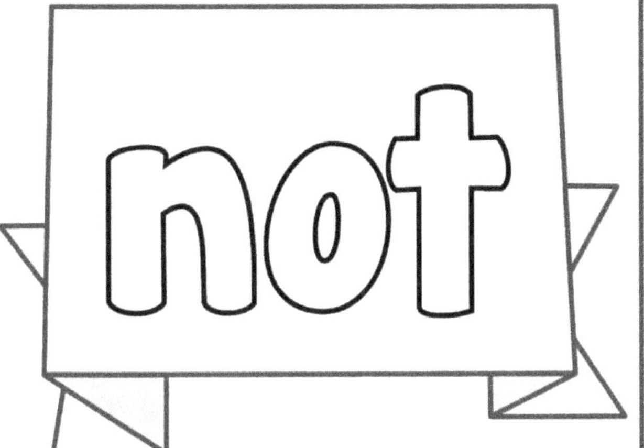

not   not   ton
ont   ton
not   ont   not
tno   not   tno

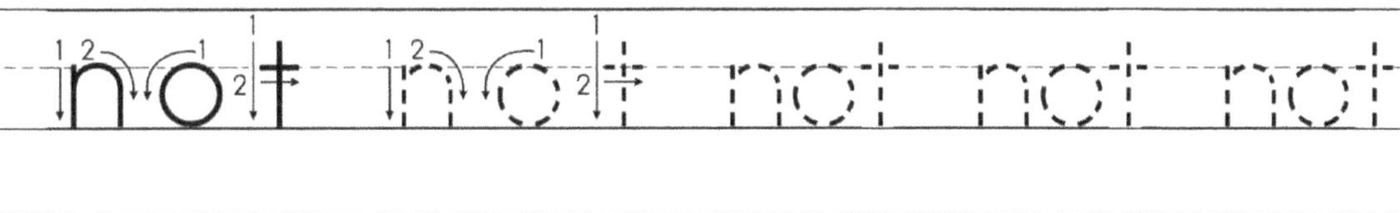
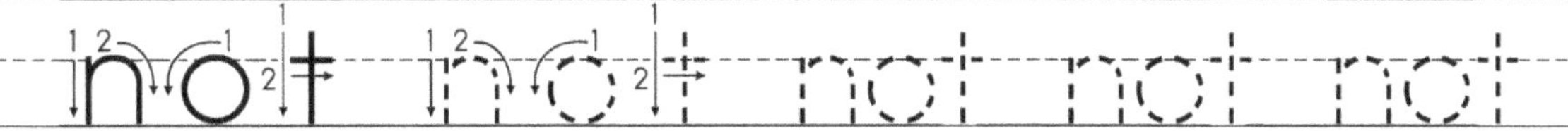

Fill in the blank with the sight word.

That is _______ my dog.

That is not my dog.

Fill in each box to make the sight word.

 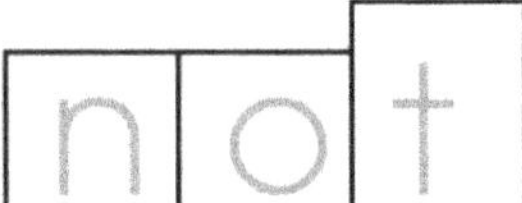 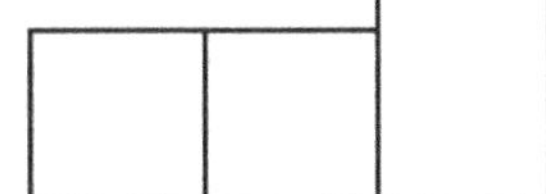 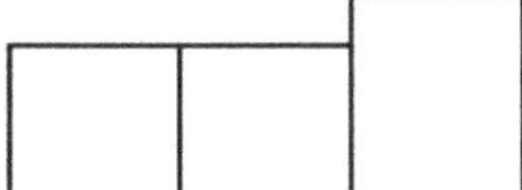

Say, spell, and color word.

Circle the correct spelling in the box.

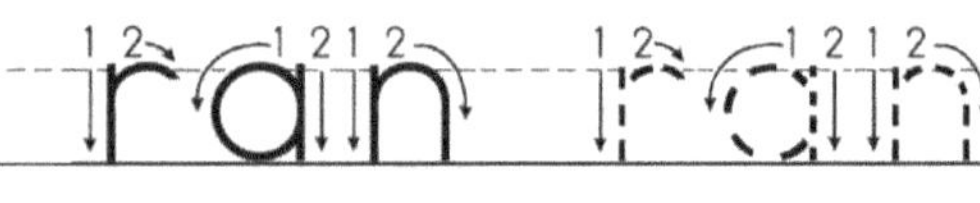

Fill in the blank with the sight word.

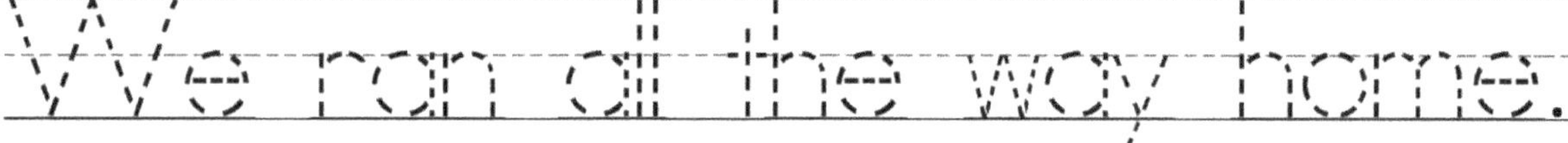

Fill in each box to make the sight word.

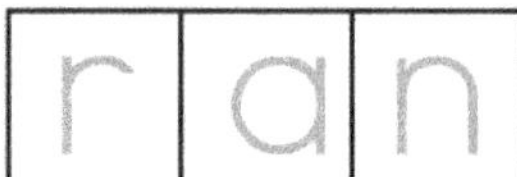
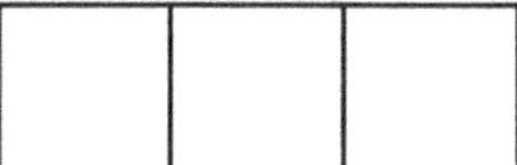
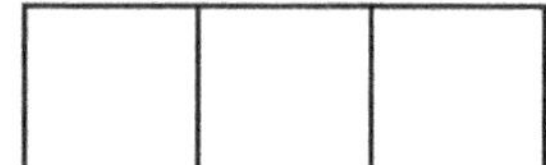

run

Say, spell, and color word.

Circle the correct spelling in the box.

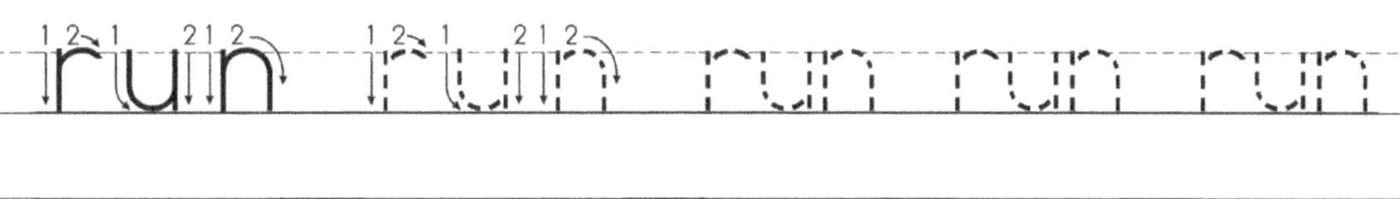

Fill in the blank with the sight word.

Fill in each box to make the sight word.

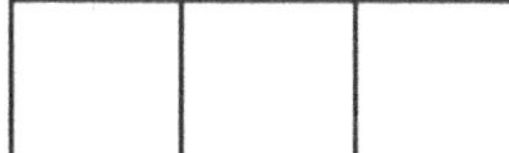

Say, spell, and color word.

Circle the correct spelling in the box.

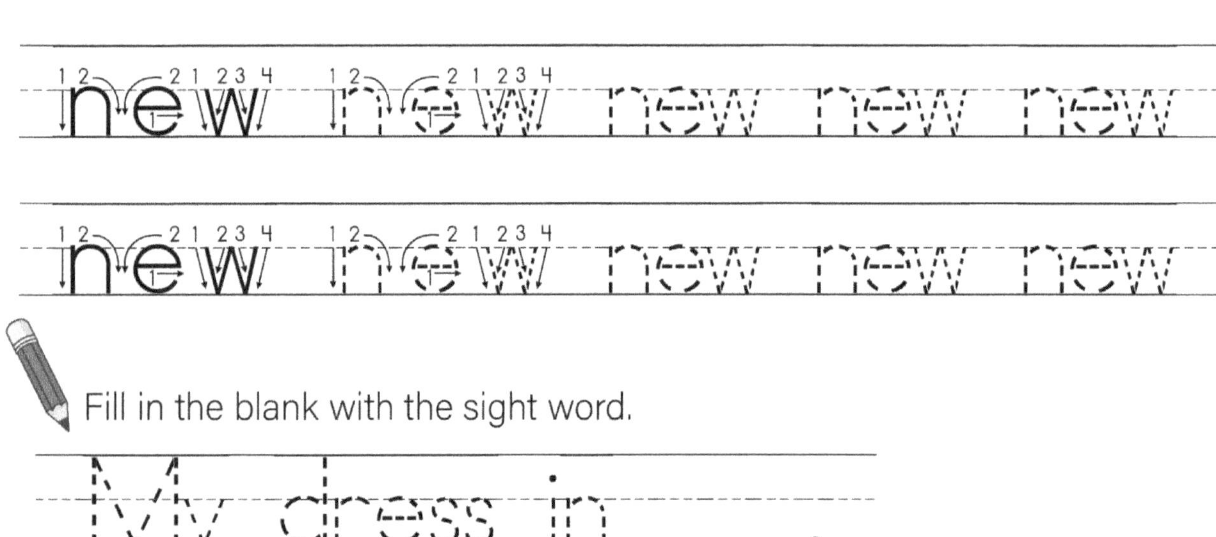

new new new new new

new new new new new

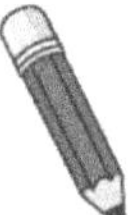

Fill in the blank with the sight word.

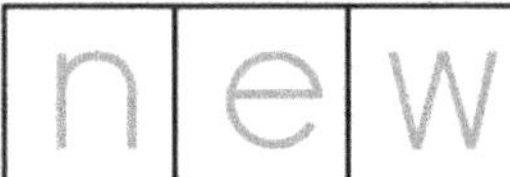

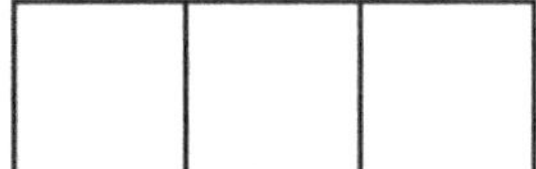

Fill in each box to make the sight word.

n e w

have

Say, spell, and color word.

Circle the correct spelling in the box.

have have have have

have have have have

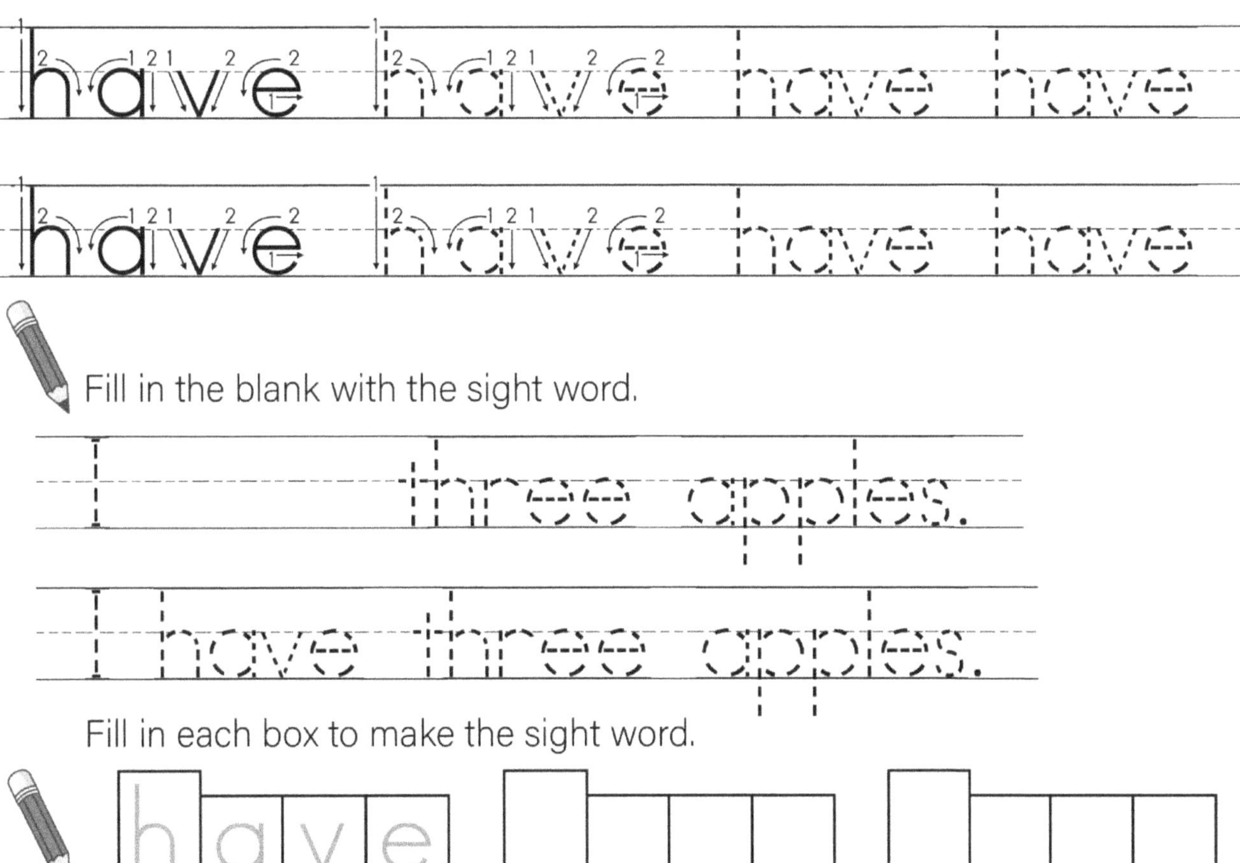

Fill in the blank with the sight word.

I _____ three apples.

I have three apples.

Fill in each box to make the sight word.

have

at

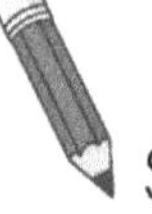

Say, spell, and color word.

Circle the correct spelling in the box.

aat   at   ta

at   ta

ta   at   at

at   att   ta

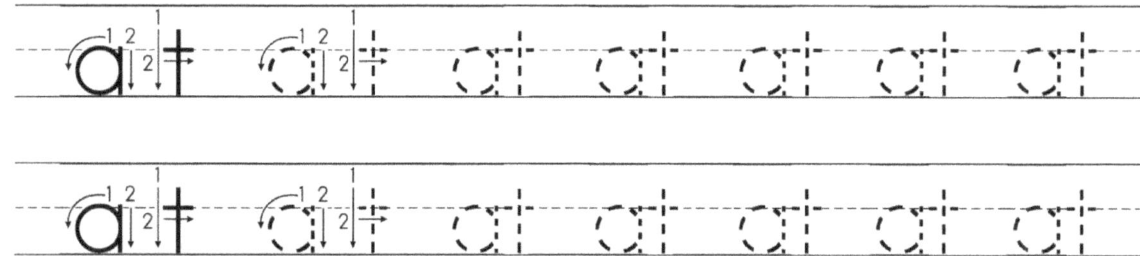

Fill in the blank with the sight word.

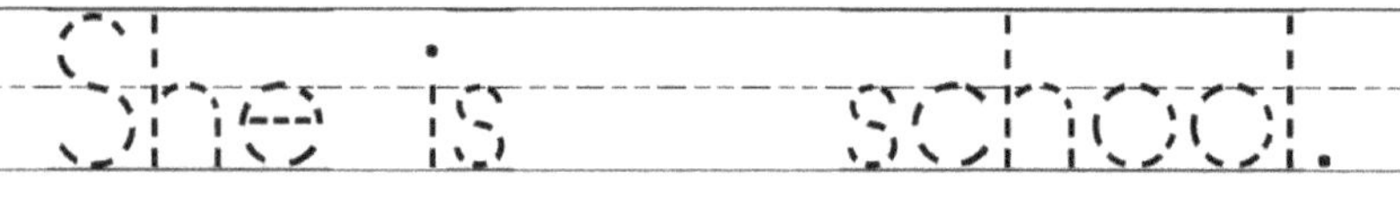

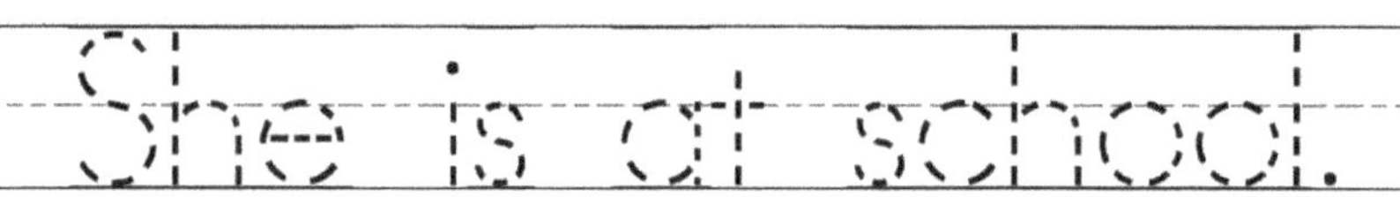

Fill in each box to make the sight word.

  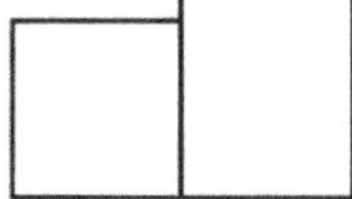 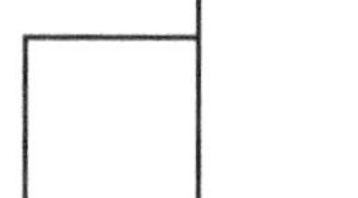 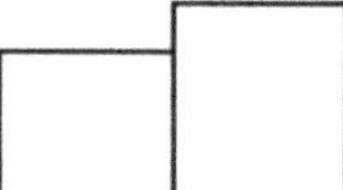